From The Streets to The Altar

An Encounter with Jesus

Tony Mejia

From The Streets to The Altar

ISBN: 979-8-8690-8619-8

Acknowledgment

I would like to express my heartfelt gratitude to God above all else. Despite not deserving His grace, He reached out and saved me. He has remained faithful even in times when I was not. I want to give special thanks to my wife, Heidy Mejia, for being my number one supporter and believing in me from the beginning. I must also mention my children, who continually bring me joy and encourage me to follow God's will. Moreover, I am grateful for my wife's daughters, who have been an incredible blessing in my life. Each one is special, and I am truly proud of them. I pray that God blesses everyone who has provided support in any way, especially those who have helped with the creation of this book. I wrote this book to bring blessings to those who find themselves trapped in a similar lifestyle to the one I once lived. It is dedicated to the overcomers and those who will experience transformation through the power of the Holy Spirit. May this book ignite a divine response in your life, and may you also bear witness to the calling of God. May it be a source of blessings to many, allowing them to truly encounter God in their own lives. May the Lord Almighty continue to bless your life and the generations to come, all in the mighty name of Jesus. Amen!

To protect privacy, the names of all individuals mentioned in my testimony have been changed to avoid any form of recognition.

CONTENTS

From the Street to the
ALTAR
AN ENCOUNTER WITH JESUS
BY: TONY MEJÍA

Prologue

When I had the opportunity to meet or see Tony Mejia, it was in the church where he delivered a powerful message. His love and passion for speaking about the wonders of God deeply impacted my life. Little did I know that as the years went by, I would encounter him again and eventually become the wife of this remarkable man whom I deeply respect and admire. Before knowing God, Tony's life was filled with temporary pleasures offered by Satan. My husband, Tony Mejia, is a testament to the power of prayer. His grandmother, Mama Luz, always believed in him and saw the calling on his life. Through her unwavering faithfulness and perseverance, she influenced my husband's life, as well as many others. Today, we witness the tangible results and the incredible power of prayer.It brings me great joy to witness and be a part of how God has restored every aspect of Tony's life. I extend an invitation to you to read this powerful testimony, which demonstrates the transformative power of God.

Heidy Mejia

Childhood Thief

I was born on June 16, 1987, in Rio Piedra, Puerto Rico. However, my parents Julio Mejia and Zelandia Mauricio are originally from the Dominican Republic. We moved to a small town called Lawrence in Massachusetts, where I grew up in an immigrant community. In this town, it was just me, my older brother Junior, and my younger sister Nana. We spent our days playing various games, such as handball and basketball, along with many other outdoor activities.

I have vivid memories of my childhood; it was truly the best time of my life. We often had cookouts, family gatherings, and big parties. Holidays were particularly special as my mom's side of the family would come together and celebrate with all our cousins. My brother Junior and I would compete in choir, and unsurprisingly, I would always end up losing and having to clean the bathroom and do the dishes while he enjoyed himself. Our parents spoiled us with the best bikes, sneakers, and clothes.

We are a family of six, with four siblings from my father's side. Junior, the oldest, lived with us, and the remaining three, Jason, Jamie, and Dailiene, who are twins, lived in New York City. Then there's me and my little sister Nana from both my mother and father. We would see each other almost every weekend. Our parents always made sure we had everything we needed materially, but one thing was missing—the love of God.

The Bible says in John 3:16, "For God so loved the world, that he gave his only Son, that whoever believes in him should not perish but have eternal life." Romans 5:8 also tells us that "God shows his love for us in that while we were still sinners, Christ died for us." And Romans 5:2-5 further states, "Through him, we have also obtained access by faith into this grace in which we stand, and we rejoice in hope of the glory of God. More than that, we rejoice in our sufferings, knowing that suffering produces endurance, and endurance produces character, and character produces hope, and hope does not put us to shame, because God's love has been poured into our hearts through the Holy Spirit who has been given to us."

Without God's love, we cannot provide the best principles for our children or the younger generation. Love goes beyond merely buying gifts or saying the words "I love you"; it requires action.

While my parents were hardworking and provided for us materially, they missed an important aspect—taking the time to sit down with us and truly listen to our feelings. They were always busy with work, and though I appreciate all they do for us, there were times when I didn't need material things; all I wanted was for my parents to play and spend time with me. I often yearned for a hug or a simple conversation with my father or mother, but they were often tired due to long working hours.

Most of the time, when my brother Junior, sister Nana, and I came home from school, our parents would still be working. This was a significant mistake on their part. They believed that if we had food on the table, a roof over our heads, and clothes and toys, it was enough. However, it wasn't. I remember Junior listening to hip hop artists like Wu-Tang and DMX, among others, who had a considerable influence on our lives.

My brother's life took a drastic turn when he started hanging out with gang members. Junior began coming home late and getting into trouble. I vividly remember the heated argument between my father and brother. Eventually, when Junior was just 15 years old, my father made the difficult decision to kick him out of the house. It was during this time that Junior became rebellious towards my father, causing them to become bitter enemies. Losing my big bro was tough for me, as he was the only person I looked up to besides my dad. I felt a great void with his absence, and it was a difficult adjustment for me to make.

As time went on, I found myself mimicking my brother's behavior. I started dressing in long t-shirts and baggy pants, just like him. My mom would try to correct me, but gradually I became more and more rebellious, albeit in a quiet and sneaky way. I acted differently at home than I did when I was out on the streets.

During that period, my parents would often sell their gold jewelry to make money. While this brought in substantial funds, it also caused a major problem that nearly cost the lives of our babysitter, my sister Nana, my mother, and myself. I still remember the terrifying incident vividly. I was only five years old at the time, and my parents were always working, leaving us in the care of a babysitter. On that fateful night, my little sister was playing with her toys in her room while I sat watching a show with the babysitter. The atmosphere that night felt different, with a heaviness in the air and chills running down my spine. I couldn't shake the feeling that something bad was about to happen.

When I dared to look out the window, I saw two men entering the building. Just a couple of minutes later, there was a knock on our door. The babysitter cautiously asked who it was, and they responded claiming to be friends of my father, named Jose. The babysitter informed them that he wasn't home, but they insisted that they knew he was on his way back from work. Although initially skeptical, the babysitter felt compelled to trust them due to their apparent knowledge of my father. She reluctantly removed the lock from the top and bottom of the door, realizing too late that they meant harm. Two men easily overpowered the older woman, and they forcibly entered our home.

Once inside, the intruders grabbed the babysitter and threatened her with a gun. I was terrified, and my little sister Nana cried out in fear. Summoning my courage, I mustered the courage to ask them if I could use the bathroom. Surprisingly, they responded kindly, assuring me that everything would be okay. But fear gripped me so intensely that I found myself unable to move. Unfortunately, I ended up wetting my pants out of sheer terror.

The robbers then locked my sister Nana in the bathroom and turned their attention to me. They demanded to know where my parents kept their gold jewelry, and I reluctantly directed them to their bedroom, pointing to the first drawer. Their disappointment was evident as they scoured the room, realizing that it wasn't the stash they were after. They impatiently asked if I knew of any other potential hiding spots, but I firmly denied having any knowledge. Their frustration grew, and they decided to wait for my mom to return from work.

Meanwhile, the robbers ransacked every room, searching everywhere. They sat me down on the same couch where I had been terrified to look out the window earlier that night. As they rummaged through my parents' room, I quietly got up and made my way towards the door. I opened it, but a voice inside me whispered, "Wait, if I leave, they might harm Nana." So, I silently returned to the couch, determined to protect my sister.

The phone suddenly rang. It was my mom calling, but the robbers had warned the babysitter, "Act normal or I will kill you." So, that's exactly what she did. It was around 11:30 pm, and my mom was on her way home. I was filled with fear, dreading what they might do to her. Once my mom entered the house, they immediately seized her and gagged her, tying her to a chair. In that moment, I feared for my mom's life. However, they quickly took the jewelry they had been searching for from her purse and fled.

Finally, it was over, and no one was hurt. The babysitter helped my mom untie herself, and she immediately began making phone calls. My father arrived from work within minutes. My mom's cousins came rushing over armed with bats, knives, and guns, but the robbers had already escaped. Just when we believed it was all over, my mom received a call from the Dominican Republic. She answered, only to hear her sister sobbing on the other end. Through loud cries, my aunt revealed, "Dad just passed away." My mom, already shattered from the robbery, was now completely devastated by this tragic news.

Living Lies

When I was 9 years old, there was a small group of kids from the neighborhood that would rollerblade, ride bikes, and go down hills. We were quite creative and used milk cartons, breaking the bottom, and nailing them to a tree to play basketball. We even built a clubhouse by the tree, which had a secret code to gain entry.

My parents were close to the Diaz family, consisting of three brothers: James, the oldest, Joe, the middle brother, and Gio, the youngest. We were more than just friends; we were like brothers. I would often sleep over at their house, play video games, and sometimes we would even play pranks on each other by stealing and marking our toys. We would also run around buildings playing hide-and-seek, always getting into some kind of trouble.

I was always seen as the black sheep of the group. I looked up to my brother, Junior, and wanted to follow in his footsteps. By now, I was 13 years old, and at school, I wanted to be part of the popular crowd. They loved me because I was funny and cool. However, my desire to fit in led me to misbehave in class, becoming the class clown and earning detention. It was during this time that I started to become curious about trying things I knew I shouldn't. For me, everything started with a lie.

Some of my friends were smoking cigarettes and marijuana, and I would try to fit in by saying, "I smoke weed too," even though I never had. They would share stories about hanging out with girls, drinking, and partying on weekends. Since I couldn't relate, I would pretend I did those things too, making up fake stories to make them think I was just like them.

One day, I was invited to hang out with some friends from school, and they started rolling a joint of marijuana. They assumed I smoked too and asked me to join. I had to keep up with my lie and said, "Of course, pass that." I had no idea what I was doing, but I followed their lead and inhaled the smoke. I started coughing uncontrollably, and they laughed, saying, "That's some good weed." I played it cool, but deep down, I had no clue and just went with the flow.

After we finished smoking, I felt my eyes grow heavy and my body relax. I also had intense cravings for food, which they called "munchies." As we continued hanging out, conversations flowed, and laughter filled the room. It was a memorable experience, bursting with laughter until our stomachs hurt. That was my first encounter with smoking weed.

We decided to go to a nearby pizzeria, and for some reason, I had a strong craving for fries. I loaded them with ketchup and salt, and they tasted amazing, satisfying my unusual appetite. I couldn't deny that I enjoyed the entire experience. I became hooked and started buying my own weed so I could always have it to smoke with my friends. Sadly, I was blinded to the consequences and where this lifestyle could lead me.

My father noticed a change in me. One day, he looked into my eyes and concluded that I was smoking. My father had been homeless at one point in his life, so he was no fool. He was strict and worked long hours. He wasn't happy with me and confronted me about it, but I tried to brush it off, claiming I was just tired. However, he knew something was wrong and decided to observe me silently. Like any typical teenager, I acted like I knew everything. I started selling weed and began to embrace the street life.

By the time I was 16, I was a mess, getting into fights and doing drugs. I thought I was cool because the lies I had been telling myself had become reality. I learned the hard way that our words have power, so we must be careful with what we say and declare.

In my city, there was a conflict between the north and south sides. I lived on the north side of Lawrence and attended Lawrence Vocational High School. I liked the school because it prepared students for the working world, but most of us didn't take advantage of the opportunity. Our minds were already drawn towards the streets. An older person once told me, "Don't take for granted what you have," but unfortunately, that's exactly what my friends and I did. We got involved in illegal money-making schemes, dressed up to impress, and tried to pursue relationships with girls. We would skip classes, gamble with dice for money, and fights were always around the corner.

In high school, we faced issues with kids from the south side messing with some of my friends from the block, and it escalated into physical confrontations. So, we united to protect each other. It was a crazy time. Often, while hanging out on the block, the south side kids would come over to attack us, but we were always prepared. We all carried Nextel walkie-talkie phones, the quickest way to alert the homies when enemies were on our turf. Sometimes, as we were smoking and playing PlayStation, we would hear the enemies outside, and one by one, we would jump up like soldiers and rush to the aid of those under attack. We always caught the south side by surprise. Some of my friends would say, "Let's see how many we can knock out," and would come out armed with pipes and knives.

Yes, things got crazy sometimes. When the police stormed the block, we would yell, "the pigs," and run to my friend's basement. After the cops left, we would roll up a blunt and laugh about how we had outsmarted them, even though some of us were bruised and bleeding.

Now my brother Junior is involved in a gang, which brings constant problems for him. He used to hang out near the Jackson projects, where there were two guys from the south side who were his biggest enemies.

One day, a fight instantly broke out between them. As my brother was throwing punches, he was stabbed multiple times, about 6 in total. Five of the stab wounds were in his back, and one pierced his lung with an ice pick. He was bleeding internally. The police noticed the holes in his shirt and rushed him to the hospital. He was in the intensive care unit (ICU) for a couple of days. At that time, I was recovering from a severe cold. When my father received the call that my brother was in critical condition, we hurried to the hospital. The sight of my brother in that state made me feel sick and angry. My mind was filled with a whirlwind of emotions. Thankfully, day by day, my older brother started to recover. It was a close call, and I thanked God because if I had acted upon my anger, I might have made the wrong decision.

Realizing how serious the situation had become, my father began to fear for my safety. There were nights when they were scared, I wouldn't come back home or that they would receive a phone call with every parent's worst news. So, my parents came to an agreement and decided that we should move to Orlando, Florida, ihopes that the change of scenery would help me turn my life around.

Moved to Florida

The first day of 12th grade class in Orlando, we had to start all over again. Making new friends wasn't that hard for me. I knew how to socialize, but I always ended up with the same type of crowd. Sometimes you can run from your problems, but if you don't overcome your weaknesses, you will remain subject to them and stay in the same cycle. Confronting your weaknesses allows you to grow and mature.

I attended Oakridge High School, but I complained to my father, "You took me out of Lawrence to come to this school." I felt like I was in prison. I knew I wouldn't be able to finish high school there because there were a lot of troublemakers, and I knew I would be tempted to get involved. My father then talked to a family we knew from

Lawrence, Massachusetts, who was living in Kissimmee. They suggested that we use their address so that I could attend the school in their district and get accepted.

So, we did, and I got accepted to Celebration High in Kissimmee. It was a cool experience for me. I felt like I was in Disney World. I was quite different from the other teenagers in the school, but I embraced the change. I felt like I had a chance to finish high school and go to college. However, my time at the school only lasted about two months before I got expelled for getting into a fight with the son of the Osceola County senator. I didn't know he was the senator's son, but he provoked me.

In the last period class, I was walking with a girl named Melissa who became my friend. We were getting to know each other since I was new to the school. Then, the senator's son appeared with a group of girls and started making fun of me in front of them. I told him, "You don't know me," but he continued to taunt me. Filled with anger, I took off my backpack and confronted him. He was much taller than me as he was on the basketball team. He mocked me, calling me a thug, but I smiled and replied, "Alright, if that's how it is." I turned around, feeling aggravated, grabbed my backpack, and left with V to the last period class. I was shaking, ready to fight. Melissa thought we knew each other and were just playing around, but I told her, "I don't know the guy. I feel like knocking him out."

The school bell rang, and I walked out of school to see my friend, Jay. He was the only person I knew since we grew up together in Lawrence. I told Jay, "I feel like I'm going to hit someone." As I looked towards the parking lot, I saw the senator's son. I told Jay, "Hold my backpack." I ran to the senator's son's car, opened his driver-side door, and said, "Get out. We're going to fight right now." He said, "No, I was just playing around." I insisted, "No, get out now." He apologized, but I couldn't let him get away with trying to fool me in front of others. So I punched him in the face, and he moved to the other side. I warned him, Saying, "That's a warning. Don't mess with me." Then, I ran to my car, pulled out, and headed to Jay's house. We laughed about what happened, and Jay told me, "You're crazy, bro. You hit the wrong dude. He's the senator's son." I was ignorant, saying, "I don't care. You know how we get down."

The next morning, I was driving in my car, listening to some Mobb Deep and smoking weed. I noticed police cars near the office, and I saw Jay. I suggested, "Let's skip the first class. I think the cops are here for me, but let's smoke." As we sat there, I started spitting a verse I had written the night before to Jay. He said, "Yo, that's fire." A few minutes later, the cops knocked on my window and asked me to step out of the car. I complied, and to my surprise, the senator's son was with them. As we went to the office, they asked me, "Do you know this kid?" I replied, "I've never seen him in my life." Once we were in the office, they showed me the security camera footage of the day I punched the senator's son. I said, "Oh, right. He was messing with me. I told him to stop, but he didn't." They informed me that due to my actions, I had been expelled from all Florida schools just for hitting one student. My dreams were shattered.

For the first time, I believed I could make it to college, but now it had all gone to waste. His father took me to court, and I had to serve community service. He even tried to put me in juvenile detention just for punching his son. It was incredible to see what money and power could do. A single punch had wiped away my path through school. My father was furious, but I told him, "Dad, school isn't for me." I felt lost, not knowing what to do next. I asked my father to buy me a mixer because I wanted to be a rapper. He bought it for me, and I started using music to express myself.

My friends would tell me, "Yo, bro, you've got potential." So, I perfected my writing skills, creating new songs with catchy hooks every day. They started calling me Sparkz because I smoked too much. One of my friends said, "Yo, Sparkz, you're killing those tracks." In that moment, I knew I had something special. I had finally found something I was good at.

My
Life Took a Shift

What now? I was kicked out of school, and my dad told me to get a job. So, I did just that and started working as a table busser at a restaurant called Smokey Bones. It was cool, but it didn't last long. All I wanted was quick money, and bussing tables wasn't cutting it. I decided to buy a few ounces of weed to start off. I went back to what I knew best - the streets. I became a product of my environment, feeling like a failure.

I had let my mom and dad down, but my dream of getting rich through music was still my main goal. Music became my best option for success. So, I started meeting people who had the same interest. I started to get the hang of things in Florida because the south was so different from the north.

By the time I turned 18, things were picking up. I was in the studio, making music on the mixer my parents had bought me, along with a microphone. It was me and my homeboy, two Costa Ricans named Dnice and his cousin Nathan. Dnice was skilled in rapping; his freestyle was insane - he could rhyme off the top of his head. So, we started making music together. He helped me develop my lyrics and believed in me. He would often say, "Sparkz, your hooks are mad catchy."

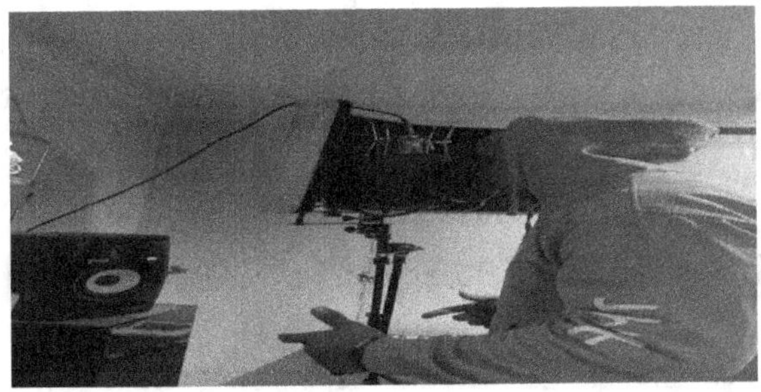

Before I started writing music, I would smoke some haze and listen to instrumentals for hours. It was as if the beats were speaking to me, and the hooks came naturally. My flow was so versatile. I started saying, "We do our own thing legit, what we're pushing is legit, we know the cops are watching, so we always stay legit. One riding with the nine and the other with the fifth, drive by on your block and empty the full clip." My friends went crazy, they were like, "Yo! That was fire!"

From there, my music started to change. People began to like my music, but that wasn't enough to start making big money. So, I found myself back in the streets selling cocaine. This was much faster than selling weed, and the money was coming in quickly. One day, I wanted to know how coke felt, so I took my first hit. I really liked it; it got me going, and I was hyped all night. Picture me, a big guy high on coke, eyes dilated, mouth swinging - I looked intimidating and crazy. Every time I used cocaine, I felt ready for anything. That drug had a hold on me; I felt unstoppable. I started with weed, ended up doing ecstasy and cocaine occasionally.

One night, I mixed them up, and I felt my heart racing so fast and hard. It felt like I wanted to go through the walls, but at the same time, I was saying to myself, "Man, I feel like my heart is going to pop out of my chest." I genuinely felt like I was going to die right there. I ran to the bathroom, pretending I was going to throw up, but nothing came out. I felt a huge relief and said to myself, "That was close."

God has given me a chance to live. He knew the purpose he had for me, and my grandmother never stops praying for us. I know that those prayers have saved me a few times in my life. I was getting tired of Florida, so I ended up moving back to Lawrence again. One of my friends named Ace, who I grew up with, came down to Florida so we could take the Greyhound all the way to Boston. The night before Ace and I started packing, we also filled up two boxes of black and mild with weed.

At every bus stop on our way up north, we had a ten-minute wait, so we would walk away from the station just to smoke. We came back smelling like straight cannabis for the entire ride. After 20 hours, we finally made it back to Lawrence.

My first stop was to the block to smoke some weed that I brought from Florida, with my close friend Fred. I called Fred, but he didn't pick up, so I yelled, "Yo Fred, open the door!" When he looked out the window, he couldn't believe it was me. He came running down and was so happy to see me. "Long time, my brother," Fred said. I asked him if he wanted to light up, and he said, "Let's do it." So, we went in and began smoking, reminiscing, and laughing at old times. We talked about some of the old fights we had with the south side boys and caught up on each other's lives. Some of our friends came to Fred's house, which was our hangout spot.

They said, "What's good, Sparks? You're back." I replied, "I miss being out here, bro, but yeah, I'm back." We started hanging out and matched up for a bottle of liquor. Fred pulled me aside and told me how crazy things were getting, then he shared the bad news about our homeboy JB. I was like, "What happened to him?" He told me, "JB's gone." I couldn't believe it. JB was one of the young ones, but he had a big heart and was straight loyal. Fred explained that our best friend Charles had killed him. I was shocked because JB was a real one. After our conversation, we went back inside to continue drinking and smoking. Once I was done at Fred's house, I went to my big bro JR's house. It was cool, but he was living with his current wife in a small apartment, so I slept on the couch.

One day, Fred called me and said the south side wanted to start a fight. So, we gathered a group of about 12 people, and when the south side arrived, they had about 15 people with them. A brawl broke out, and in the midst of the chaos, I threw a punch at one of the south side guys. Unfortunately, due to my intoxicated state, I didn't realize I dislocated my shoulder from the impact. The intensity of the situation made it difficult to feel any pain. Suddenly, the police arrived, and everyone started running. I quickly ran across the street and tried to blend in with the crowd, pretending to just be a spectator. However, the officers called me over and started questioning me.

They asked for my name, and I gave them a false one that they couldn't match. Then they asked for my social security number, which exposed my lie. They arrested me for providing false information. Since it wasn't the weekend yet, I only spent about 8 hours in custody before they released me with $40. I was charged with trespassing, and I found the situation somewhat amusing. Life on the streets was filled with excitement but also tension.

On another night, we joined forces with another gang that was also having problems with the south side. With a group of about 50 fighters, we prepared to confront our common enemies. We were drinking and getting ready, creating an atmosphere reminiscent of a football locker room. One person would declare, "We will beat up any south side guy we come across," and everyone would scream in agreement. Around 11 pm, it was time to meet the south side, so we set off.

As we reached East Haverhill Street, our groups split up, surrounding the enemies. My group positioned us on top of the hill, while the other crew was at the bottom. The south side group started coming out of a party and spotted us, immediately making some phone calls. Within minutes, they amassed a group of about 50 people as well. There were only two police officers in the street, but our numbers surpassed theirs, so we made the decision to fight. We charged towards the enemies, with pipes swinging and punches thrown. The night descended into chaos. Suddenly, police wagons started to arrive, and we scattered in an attempt to evade capture.

We were so hyped up that we went from block to block, asking random people, "What set do you represent?" People would hit us up on the walkie talkie, saying, "The enemies are here on Park Street," and we started running to join the fight. Fred got separated from us and started calling us through the walkie talkie, but he couldn't describe where he was. Eventually, he got jumped. They hit him with golf sticks and tried to throw him off a bridge, but they couldn't. By the time we finally reached him, it was too late.

Fred was badly injured and appeared to be unconscious. We kept slapping him, urging him, "Fred, don't go to sleep! Stay awake, Fred!" We made sure to take him to the hospital, which we managed to do around 4 am. It was the longest fight we had ever witnessed.

The doctors didn't take us seriously at first. Their initial questions were, "Was he drinking? Is he on any drugs?" We responded, "He had a few drinks." The doctor then said, "He'll be fine. It might be the alcohol." So, we ended up going to Fred's house, and I made sure to stay and look after him. The next morning, Fred woke up with a severe headache from the golf stick attack. We rolled up and smoked while discussing what had happened.

Moved Back to Orlando

Life was spiraling in the wrong direction. I had stopped making music and lost my focus. What now? After 6 months, I made the decision to return to Orlando. It was my second time leaving.

Things had become too chaotic for me in Lawrence. I felt stuck and wasn't going anywhere. I started fresh by reconnecting with my friends, B and Jay. They were thrilled to see me. We would hang out, smoke weed, and I would share crazy stories about what had happened up north.

Their reaction was always like, "Damn, that's wild." I began to connect with different types of people and eventually got back into selling weed. I also took up a 9-to-5 job in a roofing business, which lasted about 6 months. But deep down, my passion for music kept pulling me back. I had more stories to tell, struggles to share, and new experiences to fuel my creativity.

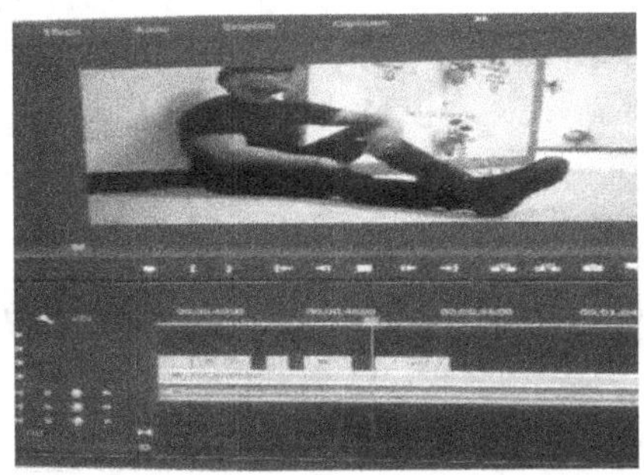

People were connecting with my music. The pain and hunger in my voice were unique, and I was truly living what I rapped about. I started hanging out with E and my cousin, Misrelies. We would spend time together.

One day, I went to a trap house to sell an ounce of cocaine. I was high and had a gun with me. After completing the sale, I received a call from my sister, Nana. She told me that she was at her friend's house and had left her iPod on the table while she went to the pool, but it was now missing. It was clear that one of her friend's roommates had taken it. I asked her where she was, and she said she was by Oakridge, giving me the directions.

Despite being high and carrying a nine-millimeter

gun, I arrived at the apartment complex and knocked on the door. A guy, who was on the phone, opened the door. As soon as he closed it, I pressed the gun to his head and demanded to know where my sister's iPod was. He claimed he didn't know what I was talking about.

My sister was in shock, never imagining that I was capable of such actions. She insisted that it wasn't him but rather the older brother. The older brother's wife came out from their room, trying to calm down the situation, but I warned her to stay quiet or else.

With the older brother still in the bathroom, I herded everyone into one room. I knocked on the bathroom door and ordered the older brother to come out immediately. As he opened the door, the gun was pointed at his face, and he stumbled back in fear. While I was questioning him about my sister's iPod, the younger brother suddenly ran out and fled the home.

I then informed them that if they didn't produce the iPod within three days, I would have my Jamaican friends burn down the apartment. With that, I told my sister we had to leave since the younger brother probably called the police. On the way home, my sister was nervous, as she hadn't expected me to act in such a violent manner or even have a gun.

My sister Nana's friend's mother called my mom's phone, but I had it with me, so I answered. She was furious, telling me, "You're going to jail for what I did." I replied, "I don't care, they took something from my sister," and then I hung up. When I got home, my mom came out screaming, tears in her eyes, asking me if I had a gun. I reassured her, "No mom, I swear I don't." My mom was trembling, saying the police were on their way. I ran to my car and sped away. I called my sister and told her to flush the drugs down the toilet because I knew they would search for me.

I drove to my friend's house at Altama Strings to hide, and thankfully, I made it. Around four helicopters hovered over my mom's house, searching for me. I was filled with nerves; life had suddenly become serious for me. My father warned me not to call any numbers because the police had tapped all the phones. My parents were broken, all their hard work to raise me seemingly gone to waste. They hired a lawyer to assess my case. Initially, he expressed concern, saying, "This is bad." He informed me that they were trying to charge me with home invasion. However, the lawyer advised me to remain low-key until he figured out how to secure a better plea deal.

I told my father that I would return to Lawrence, but I couldn't accept the possibility of facing 20 years to life. My mom spoke to the victim, and they reached an agreement never to file a report. That saved me, and my charges were eventually dropped. You would think this would open my eyes, but it didn't. I still believed I could elude a life of crime.

What's Next

My parents asked me, "What now, Tony? What are you going to do with your life?" I replied, "Buy me some clippers so I can learn how to cut hair." I felt like it was time to turn things around. I asked my barber if it would be possible for him to teach me, and he agreed. I started learning how to cut hair and eventually started working at the shop.

I remember being terrible at cutting hair in the beginning. Whenever I made a mistake, my barber would help me fix it and point out my errors. I was grateful to him for that. I became better and better with each haircut. However, it seemed like conflicts always followed me.

One day, while I was cutting a client's hair, I made a mistake, so I handed the client over to one of the more experienced barbers at the shop. I noticed the barber laughing as if he was making fun of me.

I confronted him and told him that it wasn't right. A few minutes later, he called me to the back and pulled out a knife, swinging it at me. I ran around the car, trying to avoid getting stabbed. Eventually, he calmed down and went back inside. I decided to pack up my things and leave. I felt so embarrassed, but I wasn't going to let it go like that. I went to Walmart and bought a knife and a bat.

For the next three days, I couldn't sleep, consumed by thoughts of wanting to hurt the barber. The next morning, I parked at the back of the shop and saw him cleaning his car. I wanted to attack him and poke him with the knife a few times, not too deep, just enough for him to feel it. He briefly went inside, so I cautiously approached him with the bat.

As I waited for him to come back out, my anger grew. When he finally emerged, I started beating him. He threatened to kill me, but the more he threatened, the harder I swung the bat. Eventually, he cried out for someone to help him, pleading for assistance. My friend laughed and reminded him that he shouldn't have treated me poorly a few days earlier. After several minutes, I stopped and quickly ran to my car to make my escape.

Later, my barber called me, laughing. He told me, "Sparkz, you're crazy, but that guy doesn't have any beef with you. He doesn't want any more problems." I told him it was all good, and I left it at that.

The police were called by the workers who were fixing the lights and witnessed what happened. When the police arrived, they asked about the incident with the guy I hit with the bat, but he said nothing had happened. So, I decided to move to Deltona, Florida and start fresh. There, I began cutting hair at Santi's Barbershop. I quickly gained many clients, but I was high on weed every day. It was during this time that I became friends with Wane. He had just recently been released from prison after serving about 2 years, and he was also involved in music. One day, we started freestyling together and decided to hang out. He took me to a studio he frequented. The first time I recorded my vocals on a track, everyone fell in love with it. The hook was on point. From that moment on, we formed a group called "God-like," a name suggested by the producer, Zeus. We ran with it because we just wanted to start somewhere.

We were constantly recording tracks. One day, I was hanging out with a girl outside her house, smoking a cigarette and drinking a beer. Suddenly, I noticed a big guy walking towards me from a distance. I thought he looked suspicious. As he approached, I got a bit nervous and held the bottle in a way that I could break it on his head if he tried anything crazy.

But he looked at me and said, "What's good? Let me holla at you." So, I walked towards him, and we started talking. He introduced himself as G, and I replied, "Sparkz." I could tell he was a real one just by looking into his eyes. He told me he didn't know anyone and had just arrived from New York. We instantly clicked. He had spent about 10 years in prison and held a high rank in the Bloods from New York. We exchanged numbers and started hanging out. He was wild but calm, always trying to stay positive despite his reputation as someone not to be messed with.

I moved in with a group of people, and it was chaotic. There were 3 bedrooms and 6 adults, along with about four kids. Some of my roommates were irresponsible and stopped paying, causing us to lose water. The bathroom was a mess and dirty. I had to sneak over to the neighbor's house through the back whenever they weren't home just to get some water for showering and brushing my teeth.

This was a struggle like no other. I had never experienced such hardships before, barely surviving on macaroni and cheese or a cup of soup almost every day. There was a lot of drama in that house. The couple who lived there used to argue in front of their kids, and even in front of us. It would anger me so much that I eventually moved back to my parents' house.

When I turned 18, I started working as a bouncer at a club, thanks to my friend Jean who hooked me up with the gig. Sometimes they would assign me to the VIP section, and I would puff up my chest, feeling important. We were always prepared for a fight. Jean and I were the youngest bouncers, but we were reckless.

There was one incident when the club owner

planned to beat up someone, and that was the final straw for me. I realized the problems that came along with working as a bouncer, so I decided to quit.

On one occasion, around 1 a.m., the owner would give a signal and all the bouncers would start pounding on the targeted person. It turned into chaos. Bottles were thrown, tables were flipped; it was like a storm had passed through the club. That was my last night there. I remember it was PJ's birthday, and I went to celebrate with them. They had Bacardi lemon, and even though I usually preferred dark liquor, I said, "Let's do it." I mixed the Bacardi with orange juice while Nathan rolled up a joint.

I was drinking the Bacardi like it was nothing. Dnice warned me, "Sparkz, take it easy. The Bacardi will creep up on you." But I brushed it off, insisting that I was alright. Nathan played some instrumentals, and we started freestyling. We were in the zone, feeling the flow. We decided to go to a known club to relax for a bit. I agreed, and we continued drinking.

Once we arrived at the club, I greeted some of the bouncers and went straight to keep drinking. I thought I was doing fine, or at least I thought so. Then, suddenly, I found myself sitting on the stage, looking at my watch, which read 1 a.m. From that moment on, everything became a blur.

I woke up the next day, hugging the toilet at 2 p.m., while my uncle was demanding to use the bathroom. I was in pain, everything was spinning, and my stomach felt terrible. I had never felt this way before.

My mother told me that I had called my friends to apologize, but I was confused and asked her what she was talking about. She explained that I had vomited all over my friend's car. Thinking she was joking, I called Dnice and asked him, "Hey, is it true that I vomited in your cousin's car?" Dnice confirmed it, saying, "Yeah, bro, you did, but don't worry, my cousin got it fixed."

I looked at my hands and realized that the ring my father had given me was missing. I didn't have any money left from that night; I was completely out of it. I asked Dnice what had happened the previous night and what time I had gotten home. Dnice responded, "Well, you were doing okay, you sounded drunk, but you were fine. It all went wrong when we got in the car. Your head started spinning, and you began to vomit. But we took care of you. We brought you home, stripped you down, and poured water on you from your house's water hose outside. Then we brought you to the front door and knocked. Your parents opened the door, scared and thinking something had happened to you. We reassured them that you were okay, just had too many drinks. We got home at 4 a.m."

Wow, 4 a.m.! I was shocked and felt guilty for an entire week. God had once again protected me. If my friends weren't true friends, they could've left me at the club, and I might not have been able to tell this story. But God knew that one day I would come to Him, so He kept me alive. My friends showed me so much respect, and I am grateful for what they did. That was the last time I ever mixed drinks like that.

From then on, whenever we went out to drink, I would buy a separate small bottle just for myself to control my intake. Life is short, and I have experienced a few moments where it felt like I was dying, but this time was different. I completely blacked out in a matter of seconds. I could have been gone. Lesson learned - this can never happen again. It was the worst experience.

Moved to Georgia

My father gave me a chance to come back home, setting clear rules that I had to follow. He warned me that if I broke them, I would be kicked out. At first, everything went smoothly. I was determined to do better, and I continued hanging out with the same circle of friends, hoping that things would change.

But slowly, old habits started creeping back in. I began selling weed and cocaine once again, even bringing drugs into my parent's house. Every day, when I wasn't home, my dad would inspect my room, as trust had been lost between us.

One day, I returned home, and my father called me to the garage, asking me to sit down. He placed all the drugs on the table before me. He said, "What did I tell you about this? I knew you wouldn't change, even though I gave you a chance." I replied, "I'm sorry, Dad, but this is all I know." He sternly said, "Well, you can't sell this in my house. Pack your things and leave." I responded, "I understand." Not knowing where to go, I reached out to my other brother, Jayson, who lived in Georgia. I asked if I could live with him, and he agreed, saying, "Come through." The next day, I headed to Georgia. My twin sisters were also living there, along with my brother's mother. Although we had never lived together before, it marked a new chapter in my life. Georgia was so different from what I was used to, but I found myself liking it. My sister, Daliene, and I got along well, especially since we both smoked weed. Jayson laid down the rules, emphasizing that I couldn't sell drugs there. I agreed, mainly because I didn't know anyone in the area. My brother even helped me secure a job at the check cashing store where he worked.

I was learning and getting the hang of handling large sums of money. I would always get high before work. I lasted about two months, but then I got fired because I was coming up short on cash from the register. I messed up a few times.

Now, my birthday was just a week away on June 16. I was getting ready to turn 20 years old. My sister Daliene and my sister Jamie's boyfriend Jeremy had planned to go out to a club in downtown. So, when the day came, I got ready for the night. We ended up going to the club. When we arrived in downtown Atlanta, we entered the underground club through the back entrance.

Once inside, they didn't check IDs. I was excited. There were many clubs down there, and we went to the hip hop area. We had a few drinks. At 1:30 a.m., the three of us decided to call it a night and head home. My brother Jayson didn't come with us because he was tired from a football game. When we got home, we started drinking with my stepmom, who loved me as if I were her own son.

Over time, I grew tired of living in Georgia. It was too rural for me. About six months later, I made the decision to move back to Florida. Nobody wanted me to leave, but it was time. Life was going well now. I had become a father, so I had to set a good example. My daughter was growing, and financially, things were okay. I was back at it with the music, grinding. Finally, I released my first mixtape with Wane.

We started handing out CDs to make people familiar with our music. The response from people was positive. This just fueled our hunger to make a mark in the music world. Some people were already asking when our next CD would come out because they loved our track. People were tuned in and loving our music. We spent countless hours in the studio, laying down tracks and booking shows.

My friend G was always there to keep me grounded

and focused on my music. He gave me tough love, but he saw the greatness within me and pushed me to unleash it. I was filled with confidence and would freestyle anywhere I went. People could sense the hunger in me, and my hooks were so catchy that they would instantly stick in people's minds.

Whenever we went to the club, my first move was to buy two drinks for the DJ so he would play my music. It was a strategy we used to get my music heard and gauge the crowd's reaction. While sipping on Hennessy and smoking weed in the club, suddenly I heard one of my songs playing. My friends got hyped up and started repeating the lyrics. Even those who didn't know the song were jamming to it as if they did. From that moment, I knew I had a chance.

The day of my first show was approaching, and my team and I were preparing for it. I felt nervous, but if I smoked my weed, I would get in my zone. Finally, the day arrived. We were getting ready to go on stage and found a corner to chill and wait for our turn. We watched another rapper showcase their talent, and though they were good, deep down I knew we were better. When they called us up, I pulled my hat low and stepped on stage as if I knew exactly what I was doing. For our first time, we killed it. Wane, Tone, Zues, and then it was my turn, and together we owned that stage. I could see people from the stage getting into the music and asking, "Who is this group?" We left the crowd in awe.

After our performance, we went to celebrate. It was

3 am, and we indulged in sniffing cocaine, drinking, smoking weed, and enjoying the night. Our reputation was growing, and we were gaining respect. I used to tell my mom that one day I would become rich through music, and she was happy for me but still concerned about the danger surrounding me. I was surrounded by real people, and no one dared to mess with G.

I got kicked out of Santi's barbershop when the owner saw me selling weed to someone one day. He didn't want that kind of business around his shop. So, I went to another shop called BX Cuts. It was in a great location, and I was overwhelmed with clients. The owner even gave me a key so I could close if I wanted to. There were about 10 barbers, and we were all making good money. The barber next to me, Franky, was a Christian who always talked about the Lord. I respected him, but at that time I wasn't interested in knowing God.

As we were growing in our music, there was a lot of drama within my team. We had many issues. G didn't like the video guy, Mike, because he told me not to trust him since he was only looking out for himself. Wane also had a few problems, and Zues didn't want to work with us anymore. So, we found another studio with better sound quality and affordable rates.

Wane and I eventually went our separate ways and I started working on my album called "New Direction". I went all out, recording four demo tracks to start promoting the album. I attended a support show for a group of nine rappers called KPE. They were having issues with their manager and decided not to perform that night. The manager approached me and asked if I could fill their spot since his group wouldn't be going onstage. I said, "Yeah, I'm down." I saw it as an opportunity, and I ran with it. G told me, "You're not ready, Sparkz," but I replied, "Yeah, I am. You'll see." They called me up and said, "You're next." I was ready and in the zone. I went onstage and asked the DJ to play a beat from the north and I started tearing it up.

After I finished the first song, I asked the DJ to drop a dirty south beat for the second song. The crowd went crazy, and I looked at G, who smiled. People were jamming to the music. The host went wild after my performance, and some people thought I was already famous. When I finished, I went down, and G shook my hand. He told me, "I knew you could do it. I just pushed you to the next level." After that show, I started getting more event opportunities. I had one in Orlando and killed it there as well.

At one point, people started recognizing me from previous shows. I felt on top of the world. Everything I had wanted with my music was coming to fruition. I had a few small labels who wanted to work with me, but the contracts weren't the right move. However, I remained patient because I knew my worth.

Trip Up North for 2010 New Years

I bought a 2006 Honda Accord, a 5-speed, in Lawrence, Massachusetts, even though I was living in Florida. I decided to keep the Massachusetts plates on my car. When my registration expired, I had to drive back to Massachusetts to renew it. I took the opportunity to have some fun during Christmas and New Year's with my friends and family. I enjoyed driving, so the long trip didn't bother me. This time, I made the journey to Lawrence by myself and managed to arrive in 19 hours.

Being back home was exciting for me. The delicious food and drinks, and most importantly, seeing my friends. There was an abundance of food and liquor wherever I went. My parents threw a huge party in the remodeled basement, which felt like a mini club. It had a bar, a pool table, and a dance floor where we danced to Spanish music like salsa, bachata, and merengue. We had a blast during those days, partying until 6 a.m.

During my 7-day visit, I wasn't looking for trouble, and by God's grace, I managed to stay out of it. I got my car registered, and it was ready to go. I enjoyed the company of my family and friends, and on New Year's Eve, I visited different houses for celebrations. On the last day before I was set to return down south, I was feeling high and had a bottle of Hennessy in my back pocket.

My mom called me into the room and looked into my eyes as she said, "You are going to be a preacher." I laughed on the outside, but deep inside, her words shocked me. My mom wasn't a Christian at the time, but she had been raised in a Christian household. My grandmother, a prayer warrior, constantly interceded for our family. She had even embarked on a 40-day, 40-night fast on our behalf. Through her prayers, many of us had encountered God and experienced His presence.

My uncle, who lives in Puerto Rico, was freed from alcohol addiction. He used to drink heavily, often spending the entire weekend drinking, and then resting all day on Sunday. My sister, Nana, was freed from lesbianism and embraced Christianity. I was happy for her. In addition to this, my cousin from New Jersey was diagnosed with skin cancer. I couldn't believe it. My mom told me that she was going to start treatment the day before she told her parents, "This New Year, if you guys don't drink for New Year's, come to my church with me and let's spend it at home as a family without any alcohol. God will heal me."

My cousin had great faith in God. So, my aunt and uncle agreed to follow her request. The next day, my cousin woke up and my aunt asked her how she was feeling. My cousin confidently replied, "I told you God is going to heal me." My aunt didn't pay much attention to the idea of healing, but only focused on the sickness.

When they arrived at the hospital for the treatment, the doctor performed some scans to see how the cancer was progressing. To everyone's astonishment, the doctor asked my cousin, "Where is your cancer?" My cousin calmly replied, "God healed me." The doctor exclaimed, "It's a miracle!"

Because of my uncle, my sister, and my cousin, our family came to Christ. All these extraordinary events took place during my grandmother's 40-day and 40-night fasting. For those who are praying for their family members, I declare healing over their lives in the name of Jesus. I pray that just as God broke chains in their lives, He will do the same for you.

I was shocked by these occurrences. I had always believed that God could heal, but I never truly knew Him. However, I kept this revelation to myself because I felt that the timing was not right. The next day, I gathered all my belongings, especially the weed, and said goodbye to my family.

My Encounter with Jesus

I know I wasn't a perfect person, but those testimonies impacted me deeply as I drove back down south. I was smoking, as usual, but this time my thoughts were consumed by how God had transformed some of my family members and healed my cousin of cancer. After a long 21-hour drive, I finally reached my apartment. Coming back from Lawrence felt different this time. Every day in Florida, I encountered random people talking about God, which struck me as strange. I started to realize that God was trying to get my attention. It was time for me to embrace the light.

About a week later, I arrived at the shop to start the

day. It was incredibly busy, but on this day, about five people told me that I had a calling with God. It felt like God was speaking directly to me. The day took an even stranger turn when a lady came to the shop around 7 p.m. to have her son's haircut. As soon as she entered, everyone else in the shop left. One of them asked me, "Sparks, are you closing?" I assured them, "Yes, I've got this."

While cutting the kid's hair, the lady began sharing her testimony with me. At first, I wasn't paying much attention, but then she mentioned how God had healed her husband of cancer. I was amazed. It recalled how God had also healed my cousin. I felt goosebumps and had the urge to shed tears, but I held them back. Her testimony resonated deep within me, sparking a desire to surrender, yet I knew I still had many battles to face.

She said the same words my mom had told me before I drove back to Florida, that I would become a preacher. Then she asked if she could pray for me, and I replied, "Sure." Prayers hold power, and faith can move mountains.

When I arrived at my apartment, my brother Jayson called me and invited me to his wedding. He sounded so happy as he told me about his future wife and how he had changed. He said, "I've been doing really well, bro. I started going to church with my future wife." I was taken aback. I shared everything that had been happening in my life with my brother, and he suggested, "Why don't you try going to church?"

After a long conversation with my brother, I hung up the phone and turned off the TV. I also decided to stop smoking weed. I got down on my knees and sincerely prayed to God, "If you are real, come into my life." Although it was a simple prayer, I prayed from the depths of my heart, and I felt like God heard me.

The next day, I approached my friend Franky and told him I wanted to accept Jesus. We stood in front of the shop, and Franky prayed for me. I said a salvation prayer, and tears streamed down my face uncontrollably. The Holy Spirit purified me as the tears rolled down my cheeks.

The following day, when I woke up, I felt completely different. Everything seemed brighter, and I felt lighter. As I made my way to the shop, I was filled with a profound sense of peace, something I had never experienced before. I stopped smoking cigarettes and drinking, and the transformation was instant.

Although I didn't quit smoking weed right away because I used to believe it came from the earth, one day something remarkable happened. I was in my car, smoking weed while playing some Gospel music. Suddenly, I heard a voice in my inner spirit saying, "You're destroying yourself!" It felt as if someone was there with me; the voice was crystal clear. I was nervous and shocked. I realized that what I was doing wasn't pleasing to God. I tossed the weed out of the window, and within less than a week, I was free from weed, drugs, alcohol, and more. I didn't need to go to rehab because

Jesus was my rehabilitation. It was a complete transformation. In just a week, I became a new man, something my mom had been trying to achieve in 11 years of my life on the streets. God intervened and transformed me completely. Sometimes, we need to allow God to transform people rather than forcing them.

I called my mom and said, "Mom, I have accepted Jesus into my heart. I am so sorry for causing you so much pain." I could hear the joy in my mom's voice, although she also thought I might be going crazy or playing around. But I assured her that I was serious. She was overjoyed, and tears flowed as we expressed our love and gratitude. I also spoke with my little sister and apologized for not being there for her. I explained that I didn't want her to see me in the streets, as I knew I had been a bad influence. Nana was happy about my conversion, and it was an immediate transformation in our relationship. I asked my mom for my grandmother's phone number in the Dominican Republic. When I called her, I shouted, "Grandma! Grandma! I have accepted Jesus into my heart. I now understand the songs you used to sing to me." Grandma rejoiced and exclaimed, "Glory be to God! I always knew God had a calling for you." She was grateful for this wonderful news.

Like two days after, a DJ visited the shop and the Holy Spirit spoke to me within, saying, "Watch out for his offer, the DJ is coming to see you." So, he entered and asked, "Can we talk outside?" I agreed, and once outside, he shared, "Bro, I finally got a 6-month tour, and we want you to open up for big industry artists. Plus, I have connections to help you with recordings and take you to the next level." I was taken aback, unsure of how to respond. All I managed to say was, "Hold up! Wait, I am a Christian now, I just accepted Jesus into my heart." Surprisingly, he replied, "That's cool, we can do this tour. It will give you an opportunity to preach to more people." It was a tempting offer, but I asked him for three days to pray and provide a response. He agreed to call me in three days.

The devil knew he had to try to deceive me before I grew deeper in my relationship with God. But after three days, I informed him that I couldn't accept the offer because it wasn't what God wanted for me. He was confused as he knew how much I desired success, and now that a golden opportunity had presented itself, I had turned it down. So, he left me alone.

Brother Franky disciplined me by sharing the Word

of God and helping me learn more about Jesus. Instantly, I underwent a transformation that was evident to those around me. I began preaching immediately, just like the Apostle Paul. Paul, formerly known as Saul, was on his way to imprison all Christians when he experienced a life-changing event. As he journeyed to Damascus, a bright light from heaven surrounded him, causing him to fall to the ground. In that moment, he heard a voice saying, "Saul, Saul, why are you persecuting Me?" (Acts 9:3-7).

Overwhelmed and trembling, Saul asked, "Who are You, Lord?" Then the Lord responded, "I am Jesus, whom you are persecuting. It is hard for you to kick against the goads." Filled with awe, Saul asked, "Lord, what do You want me to do?" And the Lord instructed him to go into the city, where he would receive further guidance.

The men traveling with Saul stood speechless, hearing the voice but seeing no one. Saul arose from the ground, his eyes opened, but he could see nothing. They led him by the hand and brought him into Damascus, where he remained blind for three days, abstaining from food and drink.

You see, God doesn't just call good people; He reaches out to the sick as well. There are no limitations to salvation - the key to being saved is repentance and conversion.

In Acts 2:38, Peter said, "Repent and be baptized, every one of you, in the name of Jesus Christ for the remission of sins, and you shall receive the gift of the Holy Ghost."

In Acts 3:19-21, it says, "Repent therefore and be converted, that your sins may be blotted out, so that times of refreshing may come from the presence of the Lord. And He shall send Jesus Christ, who was preached to you before, whom heaven must receive until the times of restoration of all things, which God has spoken by the mouth of all His holy prophets since the world began."

We must understand that this invitation is not based on how good or bad we are. It is for everyone who comes and surrenders their life to Jesus, for He is the bridge to the Father. This means that we all fall short of the Kingdom of God, but Jesus is the missing piece of the puzzle. I never deserved this salvation, but Jesus' sacrifice was the ultimate sacrifice so that we all could come to Him through grace, not by being perfect. If we repent and convert, Jesus will forgive us for our sins. Our sins will be cast far into the ocean and erased, and a new chapter will begin, with God writing our new stories.

I was amazed at the profound transformation I experienced. I knew I had been cleansed from everything. While everyone around me remembered my past failures, I understood what had happened to me. I had been born again through the Holy Spirit and my mind was being renewed. I found myself unable to curse anymore; my speech began to change. I would hear God's voice directing my every step through the inner promptings of the Holy Spirit, guiding me to avoid certain actions and be cautious of certain people.

The desire to smoke vanished, replaced with a longing to read the Bible all day. The allure of clubs lost its appeal, as I yearned to be in the presence of God at church. The feeling of living in my first love stages with the Lord was indescribable. I was deeply impacted by the fact that God had chosen me. However, this was just the beginning of my journey because through me, many people would be led to Jesus Christ. And the same opportunity is available to you too if you haven't made the decision to take this step in your life. God desires to use you for His Kingdom.

John 3:5-7 says, "Jesus answered, 'Truly, truly, I say to you, unless one is born of water and the Spirit, he cannot enter the kingdom of God. That which is born of the flesh is flesh, and that which is born of the Spirit is spirit. Do not marvel that I said to you, you must be born again.'"

2 Corinthians 5:17 reminds us that, "Therefore, if anyone is in Christ, he is a new creation. The old has passed away; behold, the new has come!"

Romans 12:2 encourages us to, "Not be conformed to this world, but be transformed by the renewal of your mind, that by testing you may discern what is the will of God, what is good and acceptable and perfect."

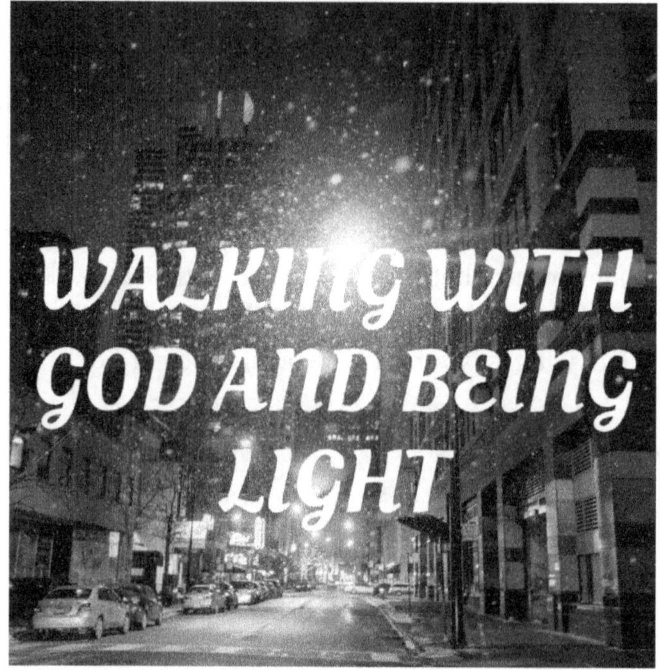

Walking With God and Being Light

Walking with God is not difficult if you surrender yourself to Him. When you walk with Him, you allow yourself to be shaped and molded by Him. That is the only way to truly know God. If the people of God had reached the promised land first, they would have never witnessed the miraculous provision of bread from heaven or the other great miracles that happened in the desert. The promised land was a land flowing with milk and honey.

Sometimes, God allows us to face challenging situations so He can reveal Himself in our lives. In a place of abundance, we may not feel the need for Him. Therefore, God may strip away everything we have in order to bless our lives supernaturally and for us to recognize and give glory to the Lord. We are called to be the light of the world, guiding others towards surrendering to God. Through us, the world should be able to clearly see Jesus.

Life will present you with many obstacles, but those obstacles do not determine your destiny. As I walk in faith, I am sensitive to the Holy Spirit, seeking to be filled and guided by Him. Now people may say that I am a good person and generous to the needy, but our goodness or works cannot erase the condition of sin. We can still sin despite our good intentions. The Bible tells us that we can only please God by living in faith and by walking in the Spirit. If we are not living in the Spirit, we are not pleasing God. The time is now, for His coming is near.

Hebrews 11:6 says, "And without faith, it is impossible to please him, for whoever would draw near to God must believe that he exists and that he rewards those who seek him."

No matter how good of a person you may be, if you don't believe in God, it won't be enough. But what is faith? Here are two definitions:

1. Complete trust or confidence in something.

2. Strong belief in God or the doctrines of a religion, based on spiritual apprehension rather than proof.

Hebrews 11:1-3 further explains faith:

1. Faith means being sure of the things we hope for and knowing that something is real even if we do not see it.

2. Faith is the reason we remember great people who lived in the past.

3. It is by faith we understand that the whole world was made by God's command, so what we see was made by something that cannot be seen.

Faith takes us beyond what we can see. As humans, we often believe in things we can see, but it becomes harder when we can't see them. However, the beauty of having faith in God is that it establishes a level of trust with Him. This is where the power of God manifests in someone's life.

There are countless testimonies of how God has intervened in people's lives, even though they've never physically seen Him. The evidence of His work is there. It all begins with faith in God, and then He reveals Himself in mighty ways to the person. If there is doubt, God's work may not be fully realized. In the Bible, there are many stories where Jesus performed fewer miracles due to the lack of faith of the people.

Matthew 13:58 states, "And he did not do many miracles there because of their lack of faith."

James 1:6-8 says, "But when you ask, you must believe and not doubt, because the one who doubts is like a wave of the sea, blown and tossed by the wind. That person should not expect to receive anything from the Lord. Such a person is double-minded and unstable in all they do."

My journey with God has become a new way of life. I no longer think, dress, or speak the same way.

2 Corinthians 5:17 reminds us that if anyone is in Christ, they are a new creation. The old has passed away, and the new has come.

Romans 12:2 exhorts us not to conform to the patterns of this world, but to be transformed by the renewing of our minds, so that we can discern God's good, pleasing, and perfect will for us.

In other words, unless I underwent a transformation of my mind by God, I wouldn't be able to understand His will for my life. Allow me to ask you a question, and be honest with yourself: Do you believe you are doing God's will? Are you certain that God has revealed His will to you? If you are unsure or not yet doing His will, it signifies the need for your own transformation by God.

This is crucial for anyone who lives according to their own understanding. It's comparable to a relationship; if you don't change certain concepts in your mind, the relationship will fail. The same applies to our relationship with God. We must start anew, taking in His teachings and seeking to walk according to His will every day, not our own.

There have been times in my journey when I relied on my own strength, but it never worked out. The things that God permits in our lives, such as businesses, work, goals, and desires, can be attained as long as God directs us towards them. Without His guidance, we will not find true success in these areas.

First and foremost, when you come to God and surrender, you are acknowledging that He takes control of your life. In that moment, you deny yourself, take up your cross, and follow Jesus. This means that you will be guided in every step along the way. As long as you let Him reveal your true purpose in life, God will bless you.

Developing a relationship with God is essential, and when you do, everything will fall into place. Don't rush it, because in walking with God, you are like a brand-new baby. You need to learn how to walk, how to please God, and how to conduct yourself. Remember, we represent God on this earth.

As Apostle Paul said in 1 Corinthians 11:1, "Be imitators of me, as I am of Christ."

Let me ask you two questions. Do you believe in God? Do you know God? I usually ask these questions because most people believe in God or some form of higher power. But let me tell you something, even the devil believes in God.

James 2:19 says, "You believe that God is one. You do well. The demons also believe and tremble." In other words, this walk goes beyond mere belief.

James 2:14-26 continues, "What does it profit, my brethren, if someone says he has faith but does not have works? Can faith save him? If a brother or sister is naked and destitute of daily food, and one of you says to them, 'Depart in peace, be warmed and filled,' but you do not give them the things which are needed for the body, what does it profit? Thus also faith by itself, if it does not have works, is dead."

The key factor here is knowing God. Sadly, the percentage of people who truly know God is so small compared to those who claim to believe but have not had a genuine experience with Him. How can you believe in something you don't know? This walk with Jesus is about having a relationship with Him so that God can reveal to you the true purpose for which you were created. Your identity is hidden in God's hands. All it takes is for you to surrender to Him.

The problem is that we often prioritize everything else before God, forgetting that everything we have is because God has allowed us to have it for blessings. We forget that wisdom, talent, intelligence, and everything good come from God.

Matthew 22:37:

Jesus said to him, "You shall love the Lord your God with all your heart, and with all your soul, and with all your mind."

Matthew 6:33:

But seek first His kingdom and His righteousness, and all these things will be given to you as well.

In other words, God is waiting for you to surrender so He can open the doors of heaven and bless your life. I cannot promise you a perfect life, but I can show you the true way through Jesus Christ. If I had continued living my old lifestyle, I would have faced challenging situations. Living to please others or living by an image or reputation can be incredibly stressful. It requires sacrifices, like any other path in life. However, living a double-minded lifestyle only creates a wall that keeps you stuck and prevents you from moving forward.

But here's the good news: you can start over; you can rise up. All you need is to give yourself to Christ, start praying, and read the Bible. The next part is challenging because you will have to evaluate and potentially cut ties with certain individuals in your circle. Why is that necessary? Well, if you want to become an entrepreneur, for instance, surrounding yourself with ambitious people who are equal to or even surpass your level of ambition is crucial.

There are two things you need to consider determining if you are surrounding yourself with the right people:

1. If you surround yourself with nonproductive people, eventually you will become nonproductive as well.

2. If you surround yourself with productive people, your competitive side will emerge, and your talents will shine bright.

As a Christian, battles will come, trials will come, and storms will come. However, the Bible teaches that the wise person who builds their house upon the Rock will never fall. On the contrary, the foolish person who builds their house on sand will face great ruin.

Matthew 7:24-27:

24 "Therefore everyone who hears these words of mine and puts them into practice is like a wise man who built his house on the rock. 25 The rain came down, the streams rose, and the winds blew and beat against that house, yet it did not fall, because it had its foundation on the rock. 26 But everyone who hears these words of mine and does not put them into practice is like a foolish man who built his house on sand. 27 The rain came down, the streams rose, and the winds blew and beat against that house, and it fell with a great crash."

I love this parable because it illustrates the importance of both hearing and applying God's words. The wise man, who puts the teachings into practice, builds a sturdy house on a solid foundation. Despite the storms and challenges that come, his house remains standing. On the other hand, the foolish man hears the same words but fails to act upon them. He builds his house on sand, and when the storms come, the house collapses. This parable emphasizes the significance of acting in our faith.

For all the mothers out there, who anxiously wait for their children to come home safely, who worry about their well-being and fear they may get into trouble, I want to encourage you to never lose hope and to put your trust in the Lord. When you commit your children into God's hands and faithfully pray for their protection, He will be their guardian through every situation. I can testify to this through my own experiences. Whenever I faced dangerous situations, I felt the shield of God's protection surrounding me, thanks to the fervent prayers of my grandmother.

Remember, receiving answers to prayer may not always come instantly. Just as my grandmother waited faithfully for 23 years to witness the salvation of seven family members, God works in mysterious ways and in His perfect timing. Sometimes, transformation occurs instantly, while other times, it takes time and molding. Each person's journey is different, depending on their willingness to surrender to God.

To those who are trapped in the gangster lifestyle, I want to tell you that there is still hope for a better future. Don't believe the lies of quick wealth and the allure of the fast life. Those promises are empty and lead to failure. Instead, invest in your future. If you are reading this book and have been touched by its message, don't stop there. Take action, just as the wise man did. Pursue your education, whether it means obtaining your Hiset (GED) if you didn't finish high school or continuing on to college. I've learned that fear can hold you back, but with God's strength, you can overcome it.

Other Books of Tony Mejia English and Spanish

1. Morning blessings & Mercies
2. A Journey to Redemption

Spanish:

1. Bendiciones y Misericordia de la Mañana
2. El Camino A la Redención

Books Written by Tony Mejia wife Heidy Mejia

1. Beyond my Wounds
2. The Power of Forgiveness

Spanish:

1. Mas Alla de Mis Heridas
2. El Poder del Perdón

From the Street to the
ALTAR
AN ENCOUNTER WITH JESUS
BY: TONY MEJÍA